PAIN AND PASSING

ISLAMIC POEMS OF GRIEF & HEALING

PAIN AND PASSING

ISLAMIC POEMS OF GRIEF & HEALING

JOEL HAYWARD

CLARITAS
BOOKS

1 2 3 4 5 6 7 8 9 10

CLARITAS BOOKS

Bernard Street, Swansea, United Kingdom
Milpitas, California, United States

© CLARITAS BOOKS 2017

This book is in copyright. Subject to statutory exception and to the provisions
of relevant collective licensing agreements, no reproduction of any part may
take place without the written permission of Claritas Books.

First Published in December 2017

Typeset in Museo 14/10

Pain & Passing: Islamic Poems of Grief & Healing
by Joel Hayward

A CIP catalogue record for this book is available from
the British Library

ISBN: 978-1-905837-50-2

DEDICATION

Kathy, my wife, you lived for me and
I will always remember your devotion
I honor you and will never forget you

Professor **Joel ("Yusuf") Hayward** is a New Zealand-born British scholar, writer and poet who has held various academic posts, including Chair of the Department of Humanities and Social Sciences at Khalifa University (UAE) and Dean of the Royal Air Force College (UK). He was elected as a Fellow of both the Royal Society of Arts and the Royal Historical Society. With the title of sheikh, he has earned *ijazas* in *'Aqīdah* (theology) and *Sirah* (the Prophet's biography). He is the author or editor of many books of non-fiction. Joel is also active in the literary arts. His first poetry collection, *Lifeblood*, appeared in 2003 to excellent reviews, and his second, *Splitting the Moon: A Collection of Islamic Poetry*, appeared in 2012 to equally strong praise. *Poems from the Straight Path: A Book of Islamic Verse*, his third major collection, appeared in 2017. His poems have also been published in many literary journals and magazines. He writes about his conversion to Islam, his religious journey, experiences and observations as a Western Muslim, hatred of extremism and intolerance, and thoughts on the state of the Ummah. He also writes more intimate poems on love, worship, and the struggle for the overthrow of the nafs. He writes his poetry to capture events each day in the way that some people keep a diary. They are therefore deeply personal, yet reflect the ever-changing world around him.

CONTENTS

Introduction	15
Dance partner	22
Last kiss	24
On a radar screen	25
So you've left me	27
Absence	28
The angel of death	30
Sunset	32
Going in	34
Buried within	36
Heartbreak	38
Wedding ring	40
Dying	43
Worlds apart	44
Diagnosis	46
Surah Al-Fatihah	48
Death certificate	50
Prayers	52
Abu Dhabi	53

Night crawls like lizards	55
Acceptance	57
Out of place	59
Your photograph	61
Inhaling her soul	63
The soul takes nothing	64
Cold prayers	66
Mon héroïne	68
Our last date	70
Unanswered?	72
A single strand	74
Emptiness	75
To be God	77
Closure	78
Those words	79
I have become a stranger	81
I am a pharaoh drowning	83
A sunlit farewell	85
The God who wasn't there	88
Pain dipped in black	92
My prayers are the best shoes	93
The inside of Houdini's milk can	96
A type of haunting	98
Woman in a wicker casket	101
Dying like pipe smoke	103

Down an empty mouth	105
A bully at the gate	107
Grab the sky and wrap her	109
Call the horizon closer	111
Inside a pearl	113
Silence is the answer	115
You will never	116
Imagine if she was Lazarus	118
Silence	120
No horizon	122
A few steps	124
Trust	126
Almost nothing of yours	128
You are not a wisp of sand	131
The key	133
My soul is old oil	134
Inside the oven	136
Dresden in a cupboard	138
The mystery of suffering	140
Stirring from winter	142
Like a legionnaire	143
A pond of carps	145
Who'd have thought?	147
In a vase	148
You have become a jewelry box	151

The language Allah speaks	153
Alone in the mosque	155
Stone circle	157
Alhamdulillah	158
The nature of grief	159
Time squeezed out	161
Life among dry bones	165
Déjà vu	167
Faith is a kite string	169
Returning from grief	172
Alone far but fearless	174
Gazelle tracks	176
Dry as sand	177
Drifting beyond	179
Truth behind a black niqab	181
Writing in the steam	183
Friday at the mosque	185
The meaning of all things	188
Ayat al-Kursi	190
Glossary	193

Introduction

Kathy died as ready for death as I could have hoped. When I say ready I don't just mean that she was so utterly broken physically and exhausted from the agony of her cancer that death would be a welcome relief. That was true, sadly, but I also mean that she had come to accept that death was close, that its approach could not be slowed, let alone stopped, and that her rapid decline and forthcoming journey into darkness were the will of Allah subhanahu wa Ta'ala.

She wasn't bitter. She and I had discussed suffering and death on many occasions. Certainly every day before death finally swallowed her on 24 April 2017 — a date that has become something of a cusp in my life — we discussed what was about to happen. She was going to die; to leave this world forever, to leave me and our grown-up daughters, to journey into Allah's kingdom, insha'Allah, there to be reunited with those of us whom Allah in His mercy might also admit. I can't say that, despite the horrific pain she suffered, she wanted to die, even after she was no longer able to talk, eat, or swallow water, but she had come to see her death as inevitable and imminent and therefore bravely and calmly steeled herself for it. She never complained. While she could still speak she asked me why I thought God was taking her now, a question I couldn't then answer and still can't.

I tried hard to comfort her. I reassured her that God has destined us all to die, and that an absence of suffering, or the achievement of old age, was unconnected to goodness. Many good people suffer and die young, and many bad people enjoy good health and long lives. I reassured her that God has promised ease and reward after death for those who are innocent of any moral wrongdoing (babies and children, for example) and those who have sought God's mercy through repentance of wrongdoing, who love Him and obey His rules, and are kind and generous to other people. By that standard, I told Kathy, she had every reason to be optimistic, insha'Allah, that God would smile upon her. She accepted this and never complained about pain or dying; not once.

Kathy's death caused poetry to pour from me and this collection came quickly. It's strange how the worst times of my life have caused these spasms of creativity. It has happened like this on at least three earlier occasions, but the horror of Kathy's pain and suffering and her departure from this world were traumatizing and brought poems more quickly than I could easily cope with. I felt I had to write; to release what was fighting inside to get out. I wrote every day, even when tired or busy, and tried to stay responsive to the poems' need for life.

So now they live, and are yours, my readers, to make sense of as you will.

I am a scholar by profession and inclination. I have to wrestle intellectually with big questions. I just have to. That's where I find joy in life; not always or even often in the finding of answers — I can't say I've found many — but in the wrestling with complex and sometimes contradictory arguments in search of deeper meaning. Following months of severe pain and physical deterioration, Kathy's death caused a great deal of fresh questioning within me about the existence and purpose of suffering. Of course, I knew what the scriptures and the theologians had to say on the issue of suffering, so I thought I'd find less to debate within myself than in fact I found. Curiously, upon further and deeper reading, I came to realize that the scriptures are virtually silent on explaining why the God who names himself the Most Compassionate the Most Merciful would cause or allow the suffering and death of good people and even innocent babies and children, and the theologians' long and twisting treatises possess not only an exculpatory tone but also flaws in logic and consistency.

These are early days in my grieving process, but I suspect that I may never find compelling and thorough answers to all my questions. Will I be able to cope with my inadequacy? Sure. I've been a believer since I was seventeen or eighteen and I've come to learn that we really cannot know much about the God we love, praise and follow. Despite His closeness to us — and the Noble Qur'an says He is closer to us than our own jugular veins — He is actually rather unknowable. Instead of being able to see and comprehend His nature and boundless capacity we are limited to scriptural descriptions of how He deals with us. As Muslims, we say that Allah has ninety-nine "names", by which we mean the titles that Allah uses in the Qur'an to describe his attributes. His attributes are perfect, of course, but, because they tend to be expressed in ways that best make sense to our limited minds, we ordinarily and unintentionally find ourselves seeing and describing God in rather human terms. For instance, God is all-compassionate. Scripture states that and I believe it, but what does that actually mean? We find ourselves usually describing how a king or queen, judge, husband, wife, parent, doctor or teacher might exhibit compassion, and then we say that God is like that, but much more of it, of course. This is clearly utterly inadequate.

I do not know why Allah the Most Compassionate the Most Merciful gave Kathy such a difficult challenge, why He did not respond in the obvious way to our constant prayers for healing, or why He made her death so wretched and painful. In my poems, as in my prayers, I have asked Him, and to date I've not received even the merest shadow of a reply. I'm not angry or offended by that silence. Who am I to demand anything of the Living God? Indeed, I have not demanded. I have merely asked questions, in the pain that accompanies grief, aware that God might or might not answer me, and that His silence is not evidence of any lack of love or compassion.

I have also asked God with what I hope is acceptable respect and deference, as befitting a peasant before an emperor, and I pray that if I've ever crossed a line I might be forgiven for the rawness of my pain. For the sake of authenticity, and poetic honesty, I have not gone back through the poems to remove any pained yelps. I have retained even the mistaken complaints I felt at the time.

I hope insha'Allah to see Kathy in Jannah, and feel enormous relief that she said her Shahada and died believing that God was whom He said He was and that He would always keep His promises. In this sense, she was indeed "ready". I wish her funeral could have been a more traditionally Islamic affair, but Kathy died in her birth city, Christchurch, New Zealand, where the burial customs are very different and where a traditional Islamic funeral was simply out of the question. I did recite Surah al-Fatihah in Arabic at the funeral and the power of God's words brought His presence close and, I think, touched everyone.

Poets love to be immersed in color, verve and pathos. The drama of life stimulates the flow of words. How sad it is, then, that during my three decades with Kathy she inspired relatively few poems. It isn't because she was colorless; an insipid woman who did not move me. On the contrary, it is because her many positive qualities ensured that our life together was relatively easy and painless. She was a peaceful, undemanding and uncomplaining wife who supported me and followed me with a calm and steady trust. However lovely that is, it's hardly the stuff of poetry. On the other hand, the day she was first diagnosed with terminal cancer ushered in an eighteen-month period of confusion, chaos, prayer, fear and trembling. Her suffering was severe and her death was a curtain falling upon a stage on which a terrible human drama had unfolded. This is the stuff of poetry, and I hope that this short and tight collection, written each and every day after she departed for the world of Allah's decisions, captures how it felt to be shipwrecked and left floating on an upturned hull. I now see the shore, alhamdulillah, but for months I saw nothing but a cruel horizon in all directions.

Pain is particular to the sufferer so I've been mindful to ensure that, although I wrote these poems during my most intense period of mourning, and some of them are clearly about one person in particular, I have tried to capture those thoughts and feelings that might also be generic; that is, accessible to anyone who is suffering, watching a loved one suffer, or trying to make sense of loss. Insha'Allah I hope that these poems, so cathartic to write, will resonate with others who are going through similar emotions.

Joel Hayward
Abu Dhabi, 2017

Dance Partner

Uselessly I watched you
glide with her
holding her tightly
while she sank into your embrace

You drew her breath
made her heart race
placed a hand upon her shoulder

It hurt

You cast me a you-can't-do-anything glance
and I winced at how light-footed you were

It was obvious
you have done this often
thief with a devilish grin
crusher of hopes

When you left with your arm around her
you looked back smugly
You're used to getting what you want
Your gloating broke me

I curse you cancer
brutal romancer
irresistible lover
damned good dancer

Last kiss

Allah the Most High drowned you
in dreams of our best times

I couldn't save you from that clutching thing
that had stolen far too much

yet I am caught in the happy moment when you
bobbed on the surface for three sunlit seconds

saw me from eyes that had closed forever,
I swear, and blew me a kiss

with a hand from your lips that had forgotten
how to sound even the smallest words

before sinking back into the depths
of the peace that enclosed you as a shroud

On a radar screen

An enemy aircraft
a black dot on a
radar screen

a trespasser
an intruder
a devil

a cancer in
my wife's lung

The size of a pea
he said
We'll watch it
he said
Don't worry

Bloody aircraft was the
first in what became
a squadron

hell-bent

soon filled the x-ray and
obliterated what we
could not protect

O Allah why do the innocent suffer?

Destroyed in a raid
broken open
she fell beneath

So you've left me

My life is a desolation
the valley of the shadow
the Sahara
an empty house

I feel you beside me in the car
wanting the window down
I can't reach for your hand
I am alone

I returned the wheelchair
Its hope was only ever a compromise
It is now just a lump in my throat

Morphine and pill bottles on your dresser
their power is a falsehood
their failure my future

Your number's in my phone
I'll never delete it
I'll never call

Absence

I know you've left
but I can't find you

I search for you in my pain
in my clever theology
in my cleverer doubts

in my silent faith
and swarming disbelief

in your lifeless hopes

and all I find are regrets
that pull my lips tighter

Sharp memories of you fading
and the cruelty of those last days
stab at me through the sheets
that wrap me in darkness

I cannot summon you
You cannot come

I stood with the toes of my shoes
in the soft soil of your grave
and my soul cried out
though you can't hear

All I wanted to say was sorry
for not always or often
being what you deserved

I said it anyway

to a filled hole

to the emptiness

to myself

So you've gone to the Lord
and that's good
but you are there
and I am here

and years may pass

The angel of death

She saw what I couldn't
In the corner near the door

where I'd hung her jacket
with no hope of its use

She pointed and asked
Who's that man?

I knew him from a black leather book
that spoke of his legend

He had swept over Egypt
and broken hearts and chains

God if only I could have shed
Passover blood for her

covered her
saved her

Stop coming, I said! Leave her!
although I knew he wouldn't

He just stood waiting
and she soon stopped pointing

Even after her eyelids became gravestones
and she slipped into night she felt him

I did too

When he stepped forward and leaned
to embrace her I didn't push him away

Take her! She's had enough!

He ended the murderous cruelty and
I breathed out

as she did

I felt them depart

Sunset

I watch you sink inside
retreat from light
from sound
from me

I watch your chest rise
faster
shallower
less

To where have you withdrawn?
some vast cathedral of confusion?
a cell with a sentence?
a single memory of warm things?

Are you with devils or angels?
with God?
with me?
alone?

It is a wall
bricks
I search for a door
I cannot enter

I cannot pull you back
hold you here
you are falling
away

I am far already
and nothing I can do
can stop the depths
reaching up to swallow you

Going in

We rushed to pack
before the ambulance came

I stuffed in a nightie, panties,
t-shirts and makeup bag

Gasping like a fish on the bed
you pointed to the hairbrush

and when I grabbed your reading glasses
you said "I'll never need those again"

a tear fell

I didn't pack that book on positive thinking
or the one on foods to fight cancer

I left them near the bottles and packets
full of empty promises

Now I've placed your glasses in a box
I'll never open in a room I'll seldom enter

and I gave your sister the sheepskin boots
I'd bought you to wear in winter

Buried within

I hate that I have become a cemetery

To visit your grave is to walk within me
and feel my pain

To find your headstone is to search
the emptiness of my eyes

Desolate and wasted
I am a field of death
and you lie deep

in the dark and stony earth
that is my nature

My father's grave is overgrown
and no-one visits

but I met his love in a care home and
she ventured in

Allah rewarded her and
pushed sunlight through the clouds

There is enough death
I want no one else inside

Lord chain the gates

Heartbreak

Without a coat I'm drenched in the grief
that falls as a winter downpour

It drips from my nose and chin
and I shiver beneath stars that play deaf when I plead

I beg them to share the secret of where
the Angel of Death took her sweet soul

Their silence kills me

They know! They must!

A hollow quietness fills the space where we once walked
talking of a future that has become a beetle on its back

The conspiring earth holds her body
but offers no words of comfort

The earth has shaken down our city
yet now minds his business

I call down to my wife
knowing she can't hear

I ask that droopy moon if she's with God and happy

He just stares

I search inside myself
but I am as empty as my faith and prayers

for a while

Even God says nothing
that I can understand

I cannot find her and I cannot feel her

I trudge in winter rain and shiver

Wedding ring

The greatest part of the universe
that my youth could afford

To her it remained the morning star
the cross on the spire
the crescent on the dome
the meaning of all things

She never took it off

to wash dishes

while soaking in the bubbles she loved

while groaning during childbirth

while sleeping under anesthetic
as they tried to cut out
that damned clawing thing

or while they burned her scarred throat with radiation

but when her hand swelled

like an inflated glove a week before
she fell into the past

I soaped it and forced it off
while she floated somewhere
unknown and insensible

and rushed it to a jeweler to enlarge

like my distress
my hopelessness
her helplessness

to give her back her glory
and meaning

She surrendered her soul before he'd finished

and lay in death with a pale indent
revealing how she'd always seen herself

It came back in a velvet bag

and I wore it myself for a needy moment

kissed it like I had her cold lips

and slipped it back on her finger
where it rejoiced at being home

Dying

She opened herself
to look inside
and climbed in
to keep warm

when death's
cold breath
touched her cheek

She wrapped herself
like a blanket
but deep inside
quiet and away
quiet and alone
she slipped
shivering
into winter

Worlds apart

You are nowhere here
and cannot see me

or the life I'll make that you wouldn't like

You are not within the hope of a new day,
the song of the wind, the glint of snow
or the sun's sigh as it lays beneath the horizon

You are not around me

I am suffocating in empty air and I know you're not
in a starlit stream or the lapping waves that
deceitfully kiss the shore near our old home

We are in different rooms in dissimilar dwellings
in worlds that never converge

except for souls forced through the ugly door
that's as thin as the thumbed pages of sacred text

I struggle in a cacophony of thoughts and busy people

You rest in the shade of a date palm
within the quieting walls of the eternal mosque

You cannot see that I ache
and lurch and gulp with grief

My regrets are an avalanche
a rockslide
a burial

Yet I live and you are gone
and the river between us
is the Amazon

I cannot see you
and I cannot swim

Diagnosis

His office shrank as he
played the Lord of the Worlds

This pretender couldn't say
"Be!" and it would

He couldn't ask a whale
to swallow a prophet

He couldn't create a dry path
through the sea of reeds

He couldn't say "Come forth"
to a cold friend in Bethany

But he announced a death sentence
and time obeyed

She fell into the darkness
that reigned upon the deep

She fell into the mouth of the leviathan

into an empty universe
into our crowded melancholy
the mystery of a decision
the embrace of the decider

Surah al-Fatihah

He read two poems and placed the
book on her coffin
before it vanished into the depths
of that ugly hole

Each poem curled into the air
as the smoke of a wizard's pipe

but faded like her life without a miracle

With a wizard's power he spoke
again and cast his words
as a moist mist across three hundred graves

Ancient words formed a prayer
in a language
unknown to the minds of those gathered
but familiar somewhere deep within

In the unpainted east of a city
named after the risen messiah

Arabic words curled around her
suspended body
and all angels bowed

"Bismillah ar rahman ar rahim ..."

The first verses of a sacred text

the opening of a door between worlds

the echo of creation's sixth day

The words drove devils back into shadows
and birds on barren branches bowed

The words drew judgment day a second closer
and the Lord enjoyed His words aloud
where they hadn't been before

in the quake-broken east of a city
named after the risen messiah

Death certificate

A death certificate opened
on my computer screen
like a white rose in a light mist

immaculate and orderly
words parading like graduating cadets

The name of that beast hidden in Latin
like a mystery from the Revelation

yet I had seen it

eating without distraction
without looking up
no interruption
a lion on a dying calf

eyes wide and realizing

I had seen your light dim
and die

and closed your lids with a moist thumb

Now words say nothing of
the ravages and the wild

the predator or the prey

I'll forward that lifeless paper to the bank
and you'll simply disappear back into
quiet emptiness and shadow

Prayers

Our forlorn prayers fell on the floor
as unfixed pages

scripture underfoot
beauty walked on and wasted
promises dirtied

but you had folded one small prayer
like a tear-damp hanky

placed it deep within your pocket

and when you inhaled all life
on the far side He asked you for it

You gave it to Him still folded

like a love note in school

and He met your eyes as He opened
and read

and smiled

Abu Dhabi

You asked me please to take you home
two days before you left

I am there now and you are
elsewhere

Here my sorrow bakes
and my tears dry without falling

I sit in air-conditioned anguish
near a mosque where I don't want to pray

You called this home and loved it here
but now you're in the cold earth

I cannot visit

On my desk your pewter camel kneels
as though he misses you like I do

O you loved to see their long-lashed beauty
by that fast road through the desert

and when I see them next I'll
remember how you
collected them in wood and metal and
pride

while my failure to bring you back
consumes me like your disease

So enjoy what God will give you:
shade and camels in families
and my father's friendship

and pray for me in the cool breeze that
blows through the open doors
of that boundless mosque

It is home

Night crawls like lizards

Night crawls like lizards
with tongues of opalescent horror

Sleep is a blanket on someone else's bed

and I jolt and gasp like she had

connected by that plastic tube
to a life finally withdrawn

Sleep is torn from my lungs
which choke on fears that
close around me as coal dust

and all I see in the dark are the
worst things she suffered

from cancer's tongues of horror

Then radiance reaches from
your woken soul
and you recite Quran over me
like a Southern faith healer

with laying on of hands

They slither away from
the light you've conjured
and I sleep O I sleep

Daylight memories appear as camera
flashes

petty poltergeists easily banished

Yet darkness always follows day
as an anxious housemaid

Memories slip their skins and crawl
from discarded scales
again where they shouldn't

Acceptance

From your bed in the ward you saw
a modest ribbon of pale sky
through a window that could
open only slightly, like your eyes

a high sky as achingly thin as the skin of your arms
bruised like rain clouds

Yellowy eyes revealed what lips never uttered

a beaten acceptance that the sky
will exist long after you do not

and your eyes fell on me like a child
rushing for a tight hug

and mine swept you up like a father
who'd failed to stop you tripping

O you patient soul who had never
asked for more or complained of less

that same sky will also stretch above my grave

but until I fall into shadows I'll never forget you

an easy companion who said little during drives
and nothing during pain

Out of place

Everything is out of place

a curiously dead wife on anyone's
bed in a city long forgotten

her soul departing from an old
people's home

lip hanging lower than it used to

new running shoes in the corner

disposable nappies next to a bra
on an unused food tray

eyeliner on eyes that hadn't
opened for days

cold skin in a room into which
the sun streamed

morphine flowing through
a tube into a life that had
left

devotion from such an
imperfect husband

who knew she'd hate her
hair like that

and stroked her fringe
back into place

Your photograph

You smile in a picture on a shelf
and whenever I pass I greet you

as a boy passing the waiting dog
that Dad had said he couldn't play with
until after homework

I salute you with a sigh that climbs
a long ladder
from a deep pain

though the Lord of all worlds
had slammed shut in my face
that most unlovely door

leaving you in pearlescent light
and me inside the shadows of a willow weeping

An eyebrow arches to hold aloft your eyes
like Chinese lanterns glowing

as they drift away
soon to fall

And no one but me will know
that I'd taken that photo on the very day
your left lung collapsed

cancer clutching like coal in a cave

Inhaling her soul

I gulped to inhale her soul
as she sighed while it spilled

as the blood of birth

and I cried at the absence of her future

I reached to catch it before it slipped away
but these sin-slick hands couldn't grip such purity

What would I have done with it anyway?
Kept it like a genie to uncork
whenever regrets weighed most?
Whenever my shame crept out?

Her soul escaped faster than I had imagined

    — though no feather fell
    or flutter caught my eye —

into a spinning growing void
in which only one word is ever said
and always in a whisper

The soul takes nothing

We can't take a thing on our
tumbling rabbit hole trip into
the opulence of recompense

Even our book of deeds exists there
before a warm breeze lifts
on that great day of winnowing

Yet you lie like Moses in a willow basket
in the depths of the earth in that dress
that made you look slimmer

Your nails are the blood of the Nile
during that failed first plague
and your eyeliner sits like Pharaoh's kohl

Nothing matters but what is written
and the grace of the All Graceful

yet a constellation of young stars
sit on your ring finger

and above your heart the name of Allah
glows yellow from a pendant like
the oil lamp of a lighthouse

Cold prayers

A shofar blown in an empty synagogue

— a pursed squeeze of ethereal meaningless

is the sound of my abject failure to pull her
back onto the boat

A choking cough in the dawn adhan
reminds me of those gasps

the sinking and the stillness
and the defeat of my best intentions

regrets climbing atop
most things when I pray

blocking the sun as they stretch and writhe

but cold prayers are better than none
and those moments pressed flat

fill my empty flask with the warmest of things

Mon héroïne

I carried something deep inside
my pocket like Frodo's ring

with the cruel gravity of Jupiter
making every step beside you
a slog through Russian snow

I never told you

I couldn't bear the thought
you wouldn't fight

and O how valiant you were!

Even that French emperor
that I have in pewter in a box in storage

would have thumped you on the shoulder

Oh tu as un cœur de lion!

yet a lion had already
clamped its teeth into your shoulder

such pain

and you fought impossibly

until you finally fell into that shadowy shaft
without knowing that I had carried a secret
for eighteen months

that you, mon brave soldat,
had only six months to live

Our last date

O how smooth you became
as though you hadn't just died
but had become as young

as when I took you to live in that
narrow red house with
squirrels on the fence

and your eyes became as blue
as I'd ever seen eyes but yours
stared at nothing

and I knew you were elsewhere
seeing things as bright
as you'd ever seen bright

while I held you like a first date
though I knew it

was our last

and cried like I had when our
girls were born
but they weren't even there when
I said

goodbye to an easy mother and
easier wife who hadn't

complained at those foolish
things in my life

Unanswered?

My prayer is as cold as her cheek when I

kissed her goodbye and the
thought that my God

who has raised Lazarus of the Four Days
because his Beloved asked

but left me unloved

inflicted her with that cruel
and tortuous death like an

East German agent with pliers
and some curved blade is much too much

to believe and my questions
fill the quiet and pulsating

emptiness of space as fully and sadly
as cold water fills a bath that

someone has forgotten to drain yet if
Al-Ghazali, Rumi and C S Lewis could not

find adequate answers then I am golden Custer
battling Indians and I must

submit for the sake of sanity
to trust that the Most Compassionate

and Ever Merciful

intends something I can't see but still my prayers

drip like an old faucet into a cold bath

A single strand

What can that single coppery strand
curled and lonely on the dresser

pulled from my brush
tell me about the way my life

will be now that grass has
begun to grow on her grave
while I'm back in that land where
grass can't grow

with a call to prayer fluttering
like a ribbon in a warm westerly

reminding me that everything
in this world and the next belongs

to the One who gave her coppery hair
that she wore long and proudly

and I'd brushed after she'd answered
some fluttering call of her own?

Emptiness

I search an empty sky
scan the horizon
between life and

the gloaming

I find you inside as shade
from this

intense heat

as a low cloud of
dripping memories

I sit in a room of paper walls
and listen

for a whisper

yet you were quiet in life
so nothing's changed

In my unspoken voice you say
no it's fine as

you did whenever I suggested
I'd do something for you

instead of for me

but now it's not fine and I struggle
beneath

such emptiness

To be God

I loathe my yearning to be
the Lord of the Worlds

for only a minute

or less

not to feed the fly-covered starving

destroy the devil's musicians in Syria

rip barbed wire from around the enslaved

cure that devouring thing

but to return you to my world
and go back to

how things were
before you left

Closure

If it's walking through a door
and shutting it behind me

looking forward
seldom back

reaching an understanding
with unruly emotions

not having the horror
and the jolting upright

when you visit at night
in swarms of the past

I'd rather suffer as I do
and still feel you're

somewhere not
nowhere

Those words

If you had seen your
own grave you

would have stopped
and read

of the love you had
always wanted

and said to me, look
that's so romantic

although I never was
and words on

a stone were
the best I could do

but God knows
— I hope you do too

that every word
came from that

good side of me
and not the other

I have become a stranger

I have watched this man who looks
a bit like me but so much

older stumble

over things that never mattered
and question the certainties that always had

I saw him scowl at the crescent moon

slide the book into that
tight gap on the shelf

ask why and why and why

and why

He told me that Allah's not
on His throne

the cosmos is as empty as his own soul

faith brings no benefit
this side of death

Foul thoughts from a stranger
who has eaten the moist fruit of providence

who has sipped the sweetest wine
that flows from the garden

I see that dreams of mountains have become
sleepless nights in a stony valley

I hear garbled cries in the dark

but I also know that among
his ashes is a warm coal ready

to welcome the Lord's breath and kindle again within him

tongues of yellow and blue belief

I am a pharaoh drowning

The Red Sea parted
and you crossed

leaving me as a pharaoh drowning

in feelings of failure but
the sunlight stabbing down

into the depths as shimmering sabers
shows me that life is

within reach with one last struggle for air

With a great gasp I am Lazarus
stepping forth blind

in a bound cloth but alive with
the hope of birdsong

and yet you're

gone O Jonah coughed up by the
Lord's beloved on sand

as golden as the celestial mosque
where you'll pray while waiting

A sunlit farewell

Lying stretched and dead
in the heat of the shallows

as a pod of lost pilot whales
beached and breathless

ten long-stemmed lilies
gleaming like porcelain

— like her purity after the
savage scouring of her soul

cast into the water
cast into the mind of God

with a cry a whisper and
a friendless thought of thanks

that she was sitting somewhere
on a distant shore

maybe waiting in the shade
with her smile that hides her teeth

I had thrown those lilies
like palm fronds beneath

the feet of Christ
entering the City of David

Hosanna hosanna

Welcome her O Allah
into Your enteral citadel

We had sat sometimes where the water
lapped beneath an all-conquering sun

but it was that worst of things
that overthrew her

Now lilies float like a fleet of
fishing dhows

where she had paddled
in rolled-up trousers

buoyed by the solitude
that always clung to this spot

Now she's beyond
and I am here

with feet in that
warm lapping death

with lilies my floating
farewell and I ask Allah the

Lord of life and death to hold
her closer than I ever had

The God who wasn't there

When she fell in battle
lanced by a grinning foe

when she arched in agony
within the clamor of combat

when she closed her eyes
and rose in a warrior's death

where on earth were you?

We had fought beneath your banner

called your name in the charge

but when the tide turned
we could not see you at the front

O Allah

Defeat is crushing and my wounds
are disfiguring

yet I live while she is gone
and the carnage is grotesque

Were you anywhere while
she writhed?

Where were you when she
slipped from her chain mail

and became a memory?

I am not so foolish to imagine
that I understand war

I am not so foolish to think
I understand death

My General

And you say that even in defeat
a victory has occurred

a soul has been restored
though the courage of battle

the scourging and scouring

the prayers for salvation

O my General all I see is a
pyrrhic victory

I feel the pain of subjugation

Today is a new day
and I am warmed

You are inspecting the guard
and I am at attention

Emperor of emperors you exalt me
with a medal

my part was small while hers was
beyond all bravery

You pass before me and I increase
and will march again beneath your banner

Pain dipped in black

You dipped your words
in gold and hung them

across the sky to dry

You soaked your prayers
in tears and flung them up

droplets fell upon us
as pearls

You dipped your pain
in black and left it hidden

beneath the stairs

and I can follow a trail
of drips leading to the

bed where you died on sheets
as white as Greek cliffs

My prayers are the best shoes

My prayers are the best
shoes for walking

Long hikes in dark places
seem shorter when feet don't hurt

My quietest whispers are the
best cloak to keep out the

deadening winds of despair

But in what can I clothe myself
when doubt is a downpour?

Or disbelief? O Allah no!

I feel as naked and ashamed
as Adam listening to the

Lord in the Garden

This cursed clever mind that
questions the unquestionable

lifts cushions to see what's
on the couch beneath

looks behind the couch to
see what's been hidden

pulls apart words in search of other words

and asks for evidence for what's been written

O metaphor and allegory

poetry and slippery mysteries

how I feast upon the succulent food
you've cooked and

leave the burned blackness of the literal
for those who like

a question to have only one answer

but to think that God should inflict a man with

a mind like mine is a sure sweetness and a

mind in which faith and doubt swim
in the same rip current

is the very reason why prayers
are the best shoes for this man's journey

The inside of Houdini's milk can

Death is the inside
of Houdini's milk can

of Jonah's great gulping fish
in the ghastly depths

It's being locked in a safe and
thrown overboard at night

You entered with an audience

my sister, me and ten thousand
angels singing like Anglican choirboys

or maybe I just imagined that
you meant enough to God but

I swear I heard them lift the roof
and carry your soul in the

highest notes on a journey
of fluttering ribbons

blue and red, your favorites

or mine but you always liked
what I liked but neither of us

liked what happened in those
atrocious days of April when

you knew your final illusion
would end

in a failure to escape

A type of haunting

I found you this morning in a bowl of sugar

and you came again
when I drank black tea with none

You even appeared while
I knelt praying and

took every easy thought
like a naughty girl with two dollars

in change taken from her mother's purse

You flamed as a firefly
and my closed eyes
weren't able to stop you

flitting through my thoughts like
a fantail in a forest

but if I'm honest you didn't really dance
like a bird

When I looked out to the Lord
from my prayer mat like a captain

searching for icebergs I saw

you dying in a photo on a shelf
but you'd smiled a tortured smile because

I needed a photo for a passport
I knew you'd never use

and a crushing crisis in my breathing
and a choke caused

my soul to crash down to earth
and crawl back deep within me

Flying home without you

abandoned

back there with a child's grave on one side
and a grandma's on the other

I closed my eyes while I drank bitter tea
without sugar and

thought of the haunted Heathcliff watching

waiting at the window

Woman in a wicker casket

Imagine laying this amiable woman to rest
in a wicker casket

woven from willow

like a washing basket full of damp
and lemon-smelling sheets

an outdoor chair on a soft-paneled veranda

the ark that carried Moses
on the Nile from death to life

— though her journey went
another way

and everyone agreed that
she would have loved it
because she was easy and

hated fuss and luxury
but she might have preferred

mahogany because in life

she'd always relished running
her fingers over any wood
polished like a piano

Gathered around the grave

bleak and black

we gaped into the
mouth that seemed

as deep as a descent to the damned

yet we knew that it led elsewhere

and wished this easy woman Godspeed
into the earth in a woven casket

beneath a mahogany sky that
hung like wet laundry

Dying like pipe smoke

You curled and twisted and twirled into death
like the delicate smoke of an old man's pipe

Climbing and clutching the breeze
you faded into nothing

yet clung to us as a strangely amber scent;
as the anointing myrrh of the messiah

We've walked in the wilderness
with a pillar of fire by night and a
cloud of tears by day

Memories are manna and we have eaten
ravenously wanting the taste to last

bittersweet and full of golden calves
and plagues and snakes eating snakes and

a sun that rises every dawn
but has fallen into mourning

and a blood moon that sings psalms
and lights your path

O and it's straight and you skip
like Dorothy on yellow

So you've gone on ahead;
crossed the Jordan
with seven steady steps

reached the emerald city and
bathed in light upon light

while we in the desert sit cross-legged
and think of a river of red
and flies and frogs and

dream of locusts and our loss
and the joy of your passover

Down an open mouth

Down an open mouth, down a drain
that empties elsewhere

Disappearing, dissolving
dying is the falling and forgetting

Death is the frightening forever

Forgiving forgiving in readiness
of whatever waits

Whatever judges whatever happens

Death is horror and midnight

madness blood sadness

Horror horror the body has stopped

the hands of the clock

Time ran out of time and

nothing moves a muscle

Cancer a gunfighter
quick draw of the devil

a pearl-handled revolver
poker face and a black hat

the heavy thud into dust
ashes to ashes it's all dust

despair and decay

It's not ok it's worse than a waste
it's hard bloody hard

It's sour in the mouth bitterness
acid bile a foul taste

A bully at the gate

If death was just that tubby kid
at the school gate waiting
for lunch money I wouldn't
walk the long way around

balancing on a beam that once carried
a bridge across a creek

rather than walk through the park where
my brother broke the ice of every puddle

I am cold with bruised arm
and life is a cruel school
with teachers who turn a blind eye

Life is the slap of a ruler and the sting
of its rule

a bee crawling from my heel after
planting a flag

punishment and pain
the unfair and the intentional

The bully always wins
and I take the long way around

Grab the sky and wrap her

The moon is as thin as a tear
and as faint as a final breath

Grab the sky and wrap her head
as a soft hijab

Tighten this warm wind as
a shroud and let her float

in a dreamless sleep with
a lion's paws as a pillow

A thin moon on a thin string
hangs like a yellow bean

in that great garden where
it began with a word as

quiet as the contemplation
and calmness of creation

and when we return from this
rejected world of weakness

let that starless sky be a velvety
cloth to wipe away every stain

Call the horizon closer

My prayer is a dhow slipping the wind
and cresting the sea's great swells

I stand on the prow and call the horizon
closer closer O closer in salt air that stings

The sun sits on my hand like a sparrow
and I whisper seven selfish requests

but also something sweeter
that climbs blue stairs

In my pocket are seven coins
and I cast them into the deep

golden gleaming sinking gone

but that copper coin crude and common
is too close to the heart to throw

It becomes the moon at night and all fears
prostrate before their sovereign

except that untamed thought
that gallops over grasslands

with hooves that thud as my rapid heart

Let the agony of her death flee
from my mind! Gallop and go!

O copper moon grant me the ease
that my tears have earned

Let me sail a tranquil sea that slides beneath
in the silence of acceptance

Inside a pearl

I have withdrawn inside a pearl
and the oyster shell is closed around me
like the jaws around Jonah

Darkness upon darkness without dying

I'm wrapped in scripture like
Friday fish in newspaper

with words that testify to so much cruelty

mummified in tight rules and requirements
written for another world

O but feel the power in the psalms of the boy
who picked up five flat stones to cast only one

the parables of a wandering rabbi
and the sunlight of so many surahs

Words dance like
Salome and my mind flowers

as a garden of the sweetest colors

and even doubt or cynicism or
the groans of grief
can slither through the grass
without earning any anger

Silence is the answer

Asking for reasons is
as wise as wool in winter

as futile as trying to cling to the
dying as their descent gathers speed

An indelible silence is the echo of a question shouted
into the dome of the mosque that sits beyond

whispered into those dreams
that are clutched while waking

those elusive clouds that seem
so dark but never rain

and though cracks in the stony
valley floor widen

like those in the grieving soul
answers do not come

You will never

I am words that you
will never read

ink spilled from a well
wiped up like

blood you will never bleed

I crawl from right to left
across a white sheet

stretched on a bed made
after they took you away

I am three words unheard

and tears unseen

So I am grief and I will tarnish
every shining thing

bring age to every mirror

before I too grow old and
fall behind

and fail like the fragile
hearts I've touched

Imagine if she was Lazarus

Imagine if she was Lazarus
called out of the tomb

Or if she was the woman
who touched the hem of his robe

the earth would not have held her anyway

Now darkness reigns upon the
face of the deep

the sun has withdrawn its light
and the moon is blood

Imagine O imagine if she was Lazarus

but the power to pull the stars
from their place

to raise her even in the shadow of smoke
for the merest minutes

as Endor's witch raised the old man
before a king

is nowhere known upon the earth
and even Lazarus died again

and lies in darkness

Silence

You do not call to me as
I thought you would

You do not call

I am not Heathcliff at the window
or in the moor's damp chill

Outside my thoughts that wail like a witness
to a murder is a bludgeoned silence

the silence of ashes that
had been a fire yesterday

Extinguished! Everything that
burned is lifeless and my soul
is charred and cannot whisper

O but I had whispered to you
in those days when you stood on the edge

sweet things I said to pull you back

and then sweeter things to
make you step off

and now I say nothing because
there is nothing

and you do not call to me

No horizon

Memories are blue mountains
and for those in the valleys

there is no horizon and the sky
is squeezed into too small a space

like an unhappy rabbit pushed back
into the magician's hat

like the pain of loss when they say
it's time to get over it

The mind plays tricks
and peaks fade into the mist

and reappear more jagged
and dangerous

or as flat as the easy hills
upon which life had been lived

The mind sees what the magician
wants but truth is a chimera

and what the mourner sees
from the valley floor is always

impossible for the painter to paint
from anywhere else

A few steps

This miserable thing has cast a long shadow

a clinging twilight that hangs above
like the sagging roof of a Bedouin tent

Everyone's too noisy yet solitude
is as quiet and creepy
as a gecko climbing close

God doesn't seem interested in prayers
that barely breathe

just occasionally flop and gasp
like a fish in a boat

Words are only ink and no longer scale Everest
win wars or demand the impossible

A library of books by the ancients matters less
than a cup of tea in an unsteady hand

Yet even shadows are frightened sometimes
and shrink when threatened

and life is now a few first steps
outside the tent listening to a Prophet

say come drink and rejoice
in the companionship gifted by Providence

Sit and study again that small book
about the meaning of such large things

Trust

She died as a believer
   as beautiful in soul
      as a blue jay
         and ready
who had for years
struggled to believe
in much
   except me

The Nazarene said don't
build upon sand yet
she mistook his meaning

or wouldn't listen

and built everything upon me
and I pretended for thirty-one
years to be the rock

She saw me as Gibraltar

I knew it and tried and failed

and yet she trusted me like
an ancient prophet

I couldn't lead myself to water
much less part it

I was always Simon Peter up to my neck
and waiting for the hand of that companion

Almost nothing of yours

I have kept almost
nothing of yours
although this house

— that you never saw
and would hate
ok you'd love
the house and your
picture on my desk
but not me being
in it without you

or the life I need —

is full of you
because I fill it
as a Great Dane
in a small kennel

like water in the
baths you loved

and I flow over
the cold lip
with regret and
damned painful
memories of
your agony
and question
why

Allah

slew you like a
wolf though
you were
meek and
fearful and

I search in
every corner
for the answer
that I don't
really need
as much as
some decent
sleep

You are not a wisp of sand

You are not a wisp of sand
blowing across a desert road
dancing as a jinn

You are not dancing
anywhere as anything

Nor are you the air or in it
or the vast emptiness of
God's creation though
you're somewhere

recreated

unbreathing untalking unthinking

unliving

here where you loved camels
and I point at jinns

or anywhere where you
loved anything

yet you live and sand does
dance across the road

The key

I have no key
to let myself in.
I cannot let myself
out. Am I inside
a new life? I can't
find a light switch
and fumble forward
fearful and heavy
wondering what
happened to
everything. Am
I outside? Stuck
somewhere between
what I had and what
I want. I cannot
find the key. I
cannot find the
lock. I can't feel
a thing. No door.

My soul is old oil

A compass spins at the pole
and I am just as lost

The horizon circles like sharks
while I drift in fear of never

finding myself again. My soul is
oil draining from the sump

of that rusting car that I have
driven into the ground

black seeping weeping sinking
beneath and killing the grass

What is the mechanic
so busy with? When will he

have time to fix this worn-out
thing? Will I ever find

myself back on the road?
Yesterday the world became

a filthy smear that I tried to
wipe from my hands but

all I did was get it on my
lips. The world means so little

and I'd kick it into the gutter if
I could. Today I stuff it in my

pocket and think in the attic of the
open roads that will take me north

Inside the oven

That mad reach into the oven
to pull her out blistered
my soul like ten days in
the Seychelles I was shocked
that God had slid her into
death like something that I'd
bought on a foam tray wrapped
in plastic He had never
promised we wouldn't die but
it hurt like fingers in a vice
that she'd suffered what only
the wicked should suffer
surely yet that's the thing
even rapists win the lottery
and children die of what took
her so this world is not
where justice dangles scales like
fish just caught but she's
fine elsewhere I'm told and so
are those children but I'm here
with burned fingers and questions

that God just might
answer because no one
else can and I'm reading life
as a holy text and I finally get it

Dresden in a cupboard

Who knows what will happen
when I stand on a chair to open

the cupboard in my study where
I've crammed our life

Everything is in there. The solar system
the weeping galaxy, the

entirety of our years that passed
into nothing

crammed in without kindness
wanting to fit thirty years into

one small space so the door can
close. Behind it is Dresden

shattered bricks and bones, piles
and pyres but that's just

my heart. A long silence then sirens
shrieking and a flag

unfurled on the roof of the
Reichstag. I am defeated. Yet

deep in the bunker I remember
weddings and children and

Dad at barbecues in shorts that
were too short and you

are in there crammed shut
and in a single photo smiling though

dying on my desk watching me
write about where it's all gone

The mystery of suffering

The things they preach

those jagged jutting men who
stretch out their hands
as though they can oblige
God to reach down

and those learned scholars
arched over great tomes
trembling deep within single words

claiming truths that can't be tested

Some wrap us in a vulgar darkness
that leave us following the worst among them

Others speak of beauty and kindness
and their lamplight draws us like moths yet

none says anything deeper than a grave
about why cancer can wander like a wolf

in a maternity ward or why the pure and pious
suffer equally with the villainous

and even those scriptures that waltz
so beautifully holding truth tightly as a lover

treat with silence those very questions
about blood and burning

and the reason for it all is kept
by our compassionate creator in that place

into which we can only enter when invited

Stirring from winter

I am stirring
from a bear's
winter death
aching in
every joint and
thought. The
dripping green
scent of budding
newness has
tugged me out
of that ugly deep
and despairing
dream. I squint
into the future's
bright blueness
stretching slow
but wanting to
leave the dark
I will shake off
winter and pad
into a new day

Like a legionnaire

I have marched
parched like
a legionnaire
lost in a sea of sand

Mirages mirages
all mirages

Nothing but fire in my
eyes and skin like
the Dead Sea

stinging and I float
in the hope of a quick
death or a long life but

though I carry no mark of
a curse like Cain the smell

of pain clings like those
circling carrion things

Is everything falsehood or
madness in my eyes?

O the constellation of Capricorn
I'll reach for her and maybe just maybe

the desert will bleed into green

A pond of carps

Curious eyes stare
up from a shallow
and listless pond
of carps

A reflection
of death among
those elegant
breathless birds
swimming in
small circles

Death
in two eyes
catching
mine

a smile returned

Clouds pass
like everyone
I've known

clouds
that turn away
in times of trouble

Carps swim

beautifully
free and unaware
that nothing changes
each time they circle

I bid farewell
to death and

whispering
Allahu Akbar

destroy the mirror
with water from
a cupped hand

Who'd have thought?

Who'd have thought I
could wrestle grief and win

twist tight fingers from my throat
and breathe

pull his veiny arm
and wrench it back

step away and stare as he
hunches forward breathless

all his energy drained like a
lion that had fought to win a pride

I am unbeaten and blue bruises
will diminish

Grief will seek a weaker soul to wrestle
to the ground

In a vase

In a vase
beneath the long
stems of my failures
lies a promise made
on a Tuesday in April

I have filled every room
with their scent and
memories swirl like
a shaman's visions
brought by sweat
in smoke

In April she went to live
behind a curtain

A vase beside the bed
blossomed in blood

It is July and
hot beyond heat

here where
flowers collapse
like struggling lungs

yet possibilities live
in these bright bouquets
given to every space
where she'll never walk

I cannot break a diamond
with the heaviest hammer
but my promise is prettier
than every jeweled neck

and I remember the scar
that crossed hers cut by
a jeweler who hoped for
a salvation since denied

Flowers for another live
around me and I place
promises in every vase
hoping that a second life
can be as fragrant as the first

You became a jewelry box

You became a
jewelry box
as empty as
all that talk of
healing

and those
bedside books
on positive
thinking

The jeweler
wanted
back that
bloodstone
he'd cut

and polished
with pain
upon pain
upon pain

and its glint
upon his
open hand
lights brightly
in his smiling sky

for navigation
should I ever
sail at night

The language Allah speaks

Is the language
of the Living God the
Hebrew of ugly
ingratitude

and David's giant genius

Aramaic invocations
over loaves and fish

the Arabic poetry
of the final poet who
said he never was

the tongues of
Pentecostal pleas

maybe the slow and growing
song of sunrise

maybe the thrown-open pride
of a peacock

the fall of a single feather

or the painful twists of
cancer's screwdriver

He talked with her in
that twisting whisper
and she replied in
tightening gasps

Maybe now they speak
sweetly in the easy shade of
salvation somewhere

while I sit beside a tired
and yawning shore writing poems
listening to the Arabic of
some strange silence

Alone in the mosque

So alone on a blood red carpet
in a mosque as vast as an old asylum

haunted and empty

with a thousand angels
on my right and as many
on my left

the only sound the
heavy hum of their
silent prayers

and water running
over impure hands
somewhere far

I miss her
and wish

I could have
led her all
the way

her imam

God's ninety-nine
names hang in gold
on the wall that
marks the end of
our journey together
and the beginning
of hers

alone

Stone circle

Beside a fallen sarsen stone
around which the sun once preened

throwing time into the arms of
swooning on-lookers

unbroken but useless
and pleading for resurrection

"Let me stand again; and live"

I sit an old and sapient sage
and whisper O my friend

at least you still cast a shadow

The dead do not

Alhamdulillah

Knee-deep in snow
between the barren
silver branches of
peeling birches I
called to God to listen
to snow descend
in silence, a slow ripple
of a creek's crackle,
and a grateful spill
of prayer onto the
pure blanket spread
beneath his
outstretched compassion,
and he answered
simply
yes

The nature of grief

Questions the size of
the Blue Mosque from which
confidence has been swept by a stiff broom

questions that curl like cunning clouds over
snow peaks and spill
as rain upon unready beliefs

doubts that dig ditches
and then gun down certainties
in long and innocent lines

that step with jackboots on the necks
of every uttered prayer
and twist the heels down

scatter when the fingers of a fond dawn
emerge from a black glove
and reach to hold tight

scatter as an army broken
in battle and stream away
in fear of the vengeful pursuit

Pains that tore holes in every hope loosen
like the saddle of a stallion
that has galloped in heat

and the blueness of the bruises
on the cheekbone of faith
yellows then fades while my eyes
old and finally tearless
open anew

Time squeezed out

If I squeezed
time out of a
dishcloth

would I see
a stream of
memories
fall with
the sound
of sobbing

or laughing

or the soft
and quiet
words of
friendship

maybe prayers
falling like
a summer
rain

or the girls
playing on
the swings
before they
realized that
they did not
even like
each other

or trickling
glimpses of
the years
hunched over
books that
reveal
every
secret

except why
we must suffer

and would
my heart sink
at the sight
of my
inadequate
love
barely
dripping

But I know
that I would
reach my
left hand in
to catch
at least
a few drops
and touch them
to my lips

as a kiss

from fingers
already wet
from tears

then let them
disappear
forever

Life among dry bones

Life slithers among
the dry bones of
hopes struck down

One cannot be lower
that the living
trampled underfoot

while the dead wear the
garments of glory the nakedness
of the garden

How I fear what I desire:
slipping through the ice
into the hidden lake beneath

I fear it O Lord but I want at least to
stretch my hand down

hoping to feel warm hands reaching up

O the dead beneath have it all while we
must wait scarred by a scouring wind
at the bus stop

Déjà vu

Of all the
damned places
to be within this
expanding barrenness

today I sat shrunken
outside the office
of that false prophet
tucked tightly
in his white coat

who had
two years past
given you
half that time

and I fell upon the mercy
of another doctor
who couldn't know

that my worn-out
shoulder was not
my worst pain

You had cried
and so had I
in the car
where now
I parked
in silence

Faith is a kite string

Faith is a
kite string
as slender as
a single
thread
stretching
up
into
the
silence

without
an echo
when I shout
like a caver
who's emerged
from a tight tunnel
into a roofless cavern

a thread upon

which I tied
a key as heavy
as every doubt
to prove a truth

upon which I hung
every sin as
sheets from my bed
washed clean
and billowing

upon which I sent
mournful prayers
to climb as monkeys
with tails wrapped
like curled ferns

prayers and
questions lifted
into the mind
of the one who

made the kite
from pages of

books with words
crawling
from right to left
and crying out
like a brother's blood
and praising

holy holy holy
as they pass
the throne of the
one who makes
every throne and

slender thread

Returning from grief

Everything grew claws
and hung upside down

ugly bats beneath
a broken bridge

rivers dirtied and the sea was
vomit spilling on the sand

the sky lay as pale and lifeless as
the cold film of a thin soup

or the clear skin of my grandfather's arm
the color of old Scotch tape

and flowers cast upon
the grave were themselves
ill and gasping

but every drowning soul struggles
and some are saved

reds and blues creep back into
the black and white

sunset is not a defeat

the sound of a child's playful shout
isn't always annoying

feelings frozen begin to thaw and drip

and the sight of two pigeons
squabbling like siblings

brought an easy thought
of early life to a smiling mind

Alone far but fearless

Alone in a small
bleached boat
far but fearless
the sun a drilling
dentist and
the salt of tears
the sea around

rowing in circles
seven yes seven
around the hope
that lit your mind
as a stretching beam
cast by the eyes
of a smiling future

you pulled away from us
from me from every shore
until your bow bumped
in a beautiful beat

into the lip of the land
that floats like lily pads
beyond that lonely star
at the farthest reach of
our imagination
and you took the
outstretched hand gently
and stepped ashore

Gazelle tracks

A gazelle's tracks
as tender as
her slender neck

soft steps, alone

in the sand the stars
the soul

following the call of
the One who sung her
Sheba's song

to water clearer than tears
shaded by palms and long lashes

her return a journey planned before
the Master had asked the sun to burn
the moon to mirror and both to praise

Safe and savoring the sweetness
she is home

Dry as sand

Though I seek a poem
in the quiet in dreams
of endless choking
dark and doorless
and in the day when
everyone blahs and
walks between rooms
and there is no peace
anywhere now except
for those cut down
I am dry like sand
heavy as hell below
and hot as the air
that lifts a lithe
prayer up where
gulls circle spotting
chips in the hands of
squawking children
without a care and
I am empty of
swooping words

and snatching
sagacity yet
life is running
faster in shoes
as silent as a
sub and it passes
and passes
without a greeting
or the placing
of an orange
coal on the
fire that burns
but a little
within my soul

Drifting beyond

You are drifting from the shore

and that same tugging tide has washed away the worst

of my midnight misery

A few stars have climbed spiral stairs
back into the darkness that had
shut me in a closet

Your voice is nowhere
in the wind which weakens
within me

and even the coldness
of your death is thawing
in Allah's warm breath

Why am I not pleased that
this plague of pains is
falling?

Must I feel terrors
and torments to prove
to myself
how much
you meant?

Your voice is nowhere

but I don't need to
hear it to remember

how much I owe you

Truth behind a black niqab

Truth smiles with the eyes of dawn
from behind a black niqab and walks in light
as a delicate waterfall of ink

All is imagined, but unseen beauty
captivates and this bride stretches
a slender hand to walk and softly talk

Wisdom flits from tree to tree
and sings a morning song that
brings a chorus of unseen admirers

I have sat and listened and held the hand
of comfort near a stream that cools
the mind that burned in pain

I have let the words sink into
the soul to wrap the worst of memories
in the sharpest thorns

and my eyes follow my lady's point
to the crescent moon smiling and agree
that it's the best shape for my future

Writing in the steam

Writing regrets in the steam
on the mirror is about
as useful as I can make the
clumsy hands that let her
drop from a cliff that
spilled out of a
genie bottle but

when I leave the door open
the mist fades and there
trapped and tepid I
find a face unseen
forgotten since the fall

eyes as faded
blue as my levis and
our first car

a beard daubed
in that white paint
used to cover stains

on a soul that barks
like a beagle for the rub
of its master

Washing in a basin
deep with tears
time clings as a
salty beauty
while pain flows
alhamdulillah
from open pores
clockwise down
a drain leading
nowhere but away

Friday at the mosque

It is Friday and the smell of feet
clings to the sea upon which
the pious have just sailed

The mosque is empty and
I throw my thoughts
across that blue carpet
to the mihrab decorated
like a gaudy door opening
to the next life

I am alone with their prayers
as a soft breeze and mine
hangs low as a kite
struggling for height until

I run and tug and it soars and
every Arabic word painted gold
around that arch to the afterlife
dances and claps

and Allah the Almighty
on His throne smiles insha'Allah

I am alone on a field of blue
where the hands of those who
have finished ploughing and
returned to their homes have
left long finger marks

like scratches in the dirt of
rabbits starting burrows that
they seldom seem to finish and

trembling I place my hands
onto the handprints on the
carpet of an unknown brother
whose prayer I try to imagine

Was it like mine? Thanks to the Lord
for easing the grief that had torn me
loose from my mooring

I rest my forehead where his thoughts had
focused far more than mine for so long
on the beauty of belief

and I am enveloped

The meaning of all things

The tundra thaws

Tripping on a tusk
uncovering the meaning
of all things

after digging elsewhere

desert sand scorpions
dreams dry for decades

I rip back the skin of
the earth to let the sun
warm mammoth ribs

Death is a bored yawn
over fields of bones
great white cathedrals
protruding from the wet
warmed permafrost

Among these jutting remains
small and climbing flowers
blue and purple bruises
push up from
seeds ten thousand
years dead

On the moist surface
of a thawing femur I write
the name of all names
with the finger that points
in prayer

and in that sepulcher
with seven sunrays
calling through a
complacent cloud
I say thank you

Ayat al-Kursi

Beneath the ink
of every letter
formed lovingly
by happy ants
into words
carried on
powerful necks
across the page
of a small book
is a cavernous mystery

Call out in the cavern!
Call to the One who says
Come further in!
Deeper! The silence
hides an answer!
Deeper!

In seven sentences
I am persuaded

The rebelling mind
and the damaged soul
breathe deeply
and are soothed

and a vast light
casts truth
on every wall

The cavern is full

Sages and
prophets praying
are lifted by
a soundless voice
into the great question
and invited to bow
before the
great answer

God is on His throne
and I am dancing
like a Dervish
on fifty-nine words
of a book that
keeps a secret
like a lover but
tells the truth
like a child

Glossary

Adhan	The Islamic call to prayer. It is made five times a day, ordinarily from the minarets of mosques, to remind all Muslims that it is time to pray
Al-Ghazali	Abu Hamid Muhammad ibn Muhammad al-Ghazali (1058 - 1111) was a Medieval Muslim theologian and philosopher of almost unequaled aptitude and output
Alhamdulillah	An Arabic phrase of thanks and devotion: "Praise be to Allah"
Allah subhanahu wa Ta'ala	Allah [God], may He be praised and exalted
Allahu Akbar	An Islamic phrase: "Allah is Greater!"
Ayat al-Kursi	"The Verse of the Throne" is the 255th verse of the second chapter of the Holy Qur'an. It encapsulates the transcendence, omnipotence and glory of God and is widely memorized and displayed throughout the Islamic world
Bismillah ar rahman ar rahim	A Qur'anic phrase, used in Surah Al-Fatihah and elsewhere. It translates as "In the name of Allah the Most Compassionate Most Merciful"

C S Lewis	A brilliant scholar, essayist, novelist and lay theologian, Lewis (1898 – 1963) attempted in *The Problem of Pain* and *A Grief Observed* to explain pain and suffering
Heathcliff	The haunted and tortured main character in Emily Brontë's famous 1847 novel, *Wuthering Heights*
Imam	Arabic for leader; ordinarily given to the man who leads prayer in a mosque
Insha'Allah	An Islamic phrase: "Allah willing" or "if Allah wills"
Jannah	The Garden of Paradise, the abode of Allah's beloved after death
Jonah	The common English spelling of the Jewish, Christian and Islamic Prophet known in Arabic as Yunus
Jinn	Jinns are supernatural and ordinarily invisible creatures mentioned in The Holy Qur'an as being made of smokeless fire and possessing natures and habits similar to those of humans
Lazarus	According to the Injeel (New Testament), the Prophet Isa (Jesus) restored Lazarus to life four days after his death
Messiah	A title used for the Prophet Isa (Jesus) by both Christians and Muslims

Islamic Poems of Grief & Healing

Mihrab	Usually designed like an elegant arched doorway, a mihrab is a niche at the front of a mosque's interior, pointing to Mecca
mon brave soldat	French for "my brave soldier"
Nafs	A person's inner identity; the "self" or ego
Nazarene	The Prophet Isa (Jesus)
Niqab	A face covering worn by some Muslim women to increase their modesty
Oh tu as un cœur de lion!	French for "O you have the heart of a lion!"
Rumi	Jalal ad-Din Muhammad Rumi (1207 – 1273) was a Medieval Muslim theologian, philosopher and poet whose poetry is still extremely popular today
Shahada	The Shahada ("testimony") is an Islamic declaration of belief in the oneness of Allah and the acceptance of Muhammad as his prophet. In its shortest form, the Shahada reads: "There is no god but Allah. Muhammad is the messenger of Allah".
Surah	The Holy Qur'an has 114 chapters, each of which is called a surah
Surah al-Fatihah	The opening chapter of the Holy Qur'an
Ya Allah	Arabic for "O Allah"

www.ingramcontent.com/pod-product-compliance
Lightning Source LLC
Chambersburg PA
CBHW012004090526
44590CB00026B/3870